This Bucket list belong to:

_____

_____

MW00368373

Our Bucket List Goal

Date _____ Location _____

Reason of doing this:

_____
_____
_____
_____

Actions we have to take:

_____
_____
_____
_____
_____

Our Experience:

_____
_____
_____
_____
_____
_____

Our Bucket List Goal _____

_____

Date _____ Location _____

Reason of doing this:

_____
_____
_____
_____

Actions we have to take:

_____
_____
_____
_____
_____
_____

Our Experience:

_____
_____
_____
_____
_____
_____

Our Bucket List Goal

Date _____ Location _____

Reason of doing this:

Actions we have to take:

Our Experience:

Our Bucket List Goal

Date _____ Location _____

Reason of doing this:

_____
_____
_____
_____

Actions we have to take:

_____
_____
_____
_____
_____
_____

Our Experience:

_____
_____
_____
_____
_____
_____

Our Bucket List Goal

_____

_____

Date _____ Location _____

Reason of doing this:

_____

_____

_____

_____

Actions we have to take:

_____

_____

_____

_____

_____

_____

Our Experience:

_____

_____

_____

_____

_____

_____

Our Bucket List Goal _____

_____

Date _____ Location _____

Reason of doing this:

_____
_____
_____
_____

Actions we have to take:

_____
_____
_____
_____
_____
_____

Our Experience:

_____
_____
_____
_____
_____

Our Bucket List Goal _____

_____

Date _____ Location _____

Reason of doing this:

_____
_____
_____
_____

Actions we have to take:

_____
_____
_____
_____
_____

Our Experience:

_____
_____
_____
_____
_____

Our Bucket List Goal _____

_____

Date _____ Location _____

Reason of doing this:

_____

_____

_____

_____

Actions we have to take:

_____

_____

_____

_____

_____

_____

Our Experience:

_____

_____

_____

_____

_____

_____

Our Bucket List Goal _____

_____

Date _____ Location _____

Reason of doing this:

_____
_____
_____
_____

Actions we have to take:

_____
_____
_____
_____
_____
_____

Our Experience:

_____
_____
_____
_____
_____

Our Bucket List Goal _____

_____

Date _____ Location _____

Reason of doing this:

_____
_____
_____
_____

Actions we have to take:

_____
_____
_____
_____
_____
_____

Our Experience:

_____
_____
_____
_____
_____
_____

Our Bucket List Goal _____

_____

Date _____ Location _____

Reason of doing this:

_____

_____

_____

_____

Actions we have to take:

_____

_____

_____

_____

_____

_____

Our Experience:

_____

_____

_____

_____

_____

_____

Our Bucket List Goal _____

_____

Date _____ Location _____

Reason of doing this:

_____
_____
_____
_____

Actions we have to take:

_____
_____
_____
_____
_____
_____

Our Experience:

_____
_____
_____
_____
_____
_____

Our Bucket List Goal _

_ _

Date _ _ _ _ _ _ _ _ _ Location _ _ _ _ _ _ _ _ _ _ _ _

Reason of doing this:

_ _

_ _

_ _

_ _

Actions we have to take:

_ _

_ _

_ _

_ _

_ _

Our Experience:

_ _

_ _

_ _

_ _

_ _

Our Bucket List Goal _____

_____

Date _____ Location _____

Reason of doing this:

_____
_____
_____
_____

Actions we have to take:

_____
_____
_____
_____
_____
_____

Our Experience:

_____
_____
_____
_____
_____
_____

Our Bucket List Goal ....
....

Date .... Location ....

Reason of doing this:
....
....
....
....

Actions we have to take:
....
....
....
....
....

Our Experience:
....
....
....
....
....

Our Bucket List Goal _____

Date _____ Location _____

Reason of doing this:

_____
_____
_____
_____

Actions we have to take:

_____
_____
_____
_____
_____
_____

Our Experience:

_____
_____
_____
_____
_____
_____

Our Bucket List Goal _____

_____

Date _____ Location _____

Reason of doing this:

_____
_____
_____
_____

Actions we have to take:

_____
_____
_____
_____
_____
_____

Our Experience:

_____
_____
_____
_____
_____

Our Bucket List Goal _____

_____

Date _____ Location _____

Reason of doing this:

_____
_____
_____
_____

Actions we have to take:

_____
_____
_____
_____
_____
_____

Our Experience:

_____
_____
_____
_____
_____
_____

Our Bucket List Goal _____

_____

Date _____ Location _____

Reason of doing this:

_____

_____

_____

_____

Actions we have to take:

_____

_____

_____

_____

_____

_____

Our Experience:

_____

_____

_____

_____

_____

_____

Our Bucket List Goal

_____

_____

Date _____ Location _____

Reason of doing this:

Actions we have to take:

Our Experience:

Our Bucket List Goal

Date _____ Location _____

Reason of doing this:

_____
_____
_____
_____

Actions we have to take:

_____
_____
_____
_____
_____
_____

Our Experience:

_____
_____
_____
_____
_____

Our Bucket List Goal _____

_____

Date _____ Location _____

Reason of doing this:

_____
_____
_____
_____

Actions we have to take:

_____
_____
_____
_____
_____

Our Experience:

_____
_____
_____
_____
_____
_____

Our Bucket List Goal _____
_____

Date _____ Location _____

Reason of doing this:
_____
_____
_____
_____

Actions we have to take:
_____
_____
_____
_____
_____
_____

Our Experience:
_____
_____
_____
_____
_____
_____

Our Bucket List Goal _____

_____

Date _____ Location _____

Reason of doing this:

_____
_____
_____
_____

Actions we have to take:

_____
_____
_____
_____
_____

Our Experience:

_____
_____
_____
_____
_____

Our Bucket List Goal _____
_____

Date _____ Location _____

Reason of doing this:
_____
_____
_____
_____

Actions we have to take:
_____
_____
_____
_____
_____
_____

Our Experience:
_____
_____
_____
_____
_____

Our Bucket List Goal _____

_____

Date _____ Location _____

Reason of doing this:

_____
_____
_____
_____

Actions we have to take:

_____
_____
_____
_____
_____
_____

Our Experience:

_____
_____
_____
_____
_____
_____

Our Bucket List Goal _____

_____

Date _____ Location _____

Reason of doing this:

_____
_____
_____
_____

Actions we have to take:

_____
_____
_____
_____
_____
_____

Our Experience:

_____
_____
_____
_____
_____
_____

Our Bucket List Goal ....

Date .... Location ....

Reason of doing this:

Actions we have to take:

Our Experience:

Our Bucket List Goal _____

_____

Date _____ Location _____

Reason of doing this:

_____
_____
_____
_____

Actions we have to take:

_____
_____
_____
_____
_____
_____

Our Experience:

_____
_____
_____
_____
_____
_____

Our Bucket List Goal ----------------------

Date ----------------   Location ----------------

Reason of doing this:

Actions we have to take:

Our Experience:

Our Bucket List Goal _____

_____

Date _____ Location _____

Reason of doing this:

_____
_____
_____
_____

Actions we have to take:

_____
_____
_____
_____
_____
_____

Our Experience:

_____
_____
_____
_____
_____
_____

Our Bucket List Goal _____

_____

Date _____ Location _____

Reason of doing this:

_____
_____
_____
_____

Actions we have to take:

_____
_____
_____
_____
_____
_____

Our Experience:

_____
_____
_____
_____
_____
_____

Our Bucket List Goal _____

_____

Date _____ Location _____

Reason of doing this:

_____
_____
_____
_____

Actions we have to take:

_____
_____
_____
_____
_____
_____

Our Experience:

_____
_____
_____
_____
_____
_____

Our Bucket List Goal _____

_____

Date _____   Location _____

Reason of doing this:

_____
_____
_____

_____

Actions we have to take:

_____
_____
_____
_____
_____
_____

Our Experience:

_____
_____
_____
_____
_____
_____

Our Bucket List Goal _____

_____

Date _____ Location _____

Reason of doing this:

_____
_____
_____
_____

Actions we have to take:

_____
_____
_____
_____
_____
_____

Our Experience:

_____
_____
_____
_____
_____
_____

Our Bucket List Goal _____

_____

Date _____ Location _____

Reason of doing this:

_____
_____
_____
_____

Actions we have to take:

_____
_____
_____
_____
_____
_____

Our Experience:

_____
_____
_____
_____
_____

Our Bucket List Goal _____
_____

Date _____ Location _____

Reason of doing this:
_____
_____
_____
_____

Actions we have to take:
_____
_____
_____
_____
_____
_____

Our Experience:
_____
_____
_____
_____
_____
_____

Our Bucket List Goal _____
_____

Date _____ Location _____

Reason of doing this:
_____
_____
_____
_____

Actions we have to take:
_____
_____
_____
_____
_____
_____

Our Experience:
_____
_____
_____
_____
_____
_____

Our Bucket List Goal _____

_____

Date _____ Location _____

Reason of doing this:

_____
_____
_____
_____

Actions we have to take:

_____
_____
_____
_____
_____
_____

Our Experience:

_____
_____
_____
_____
_____
_____

Our Bucket List Goal ....
....

Date .... Location ....

Reason of doing this:

Actions we have to take:

Our Experience:

Our Bucket List Goal

_____

_____

Date _____ Location _____

Reason of doing this:

_____

_____

_____

_____

Actions we have to take:

_____

_____

_____

_____

_____

_____

Our Experience:

_____

_____

_____

_____

_____

_____

Our Bucket List Goal

Date _____ Location _____

Reason of doing this:

_____
_____
_____
_____

Actions we have to take:

_____
_____
_____
_____
_____
_____

Our Experience:

_____
_____
_____
_____
_____

Our Bucket List Goal _____
_____

Date _____ Location _____

Reason of doing this:
_____
_____
_____
_____

Actions we have to take:
_____
_____
_____
_____
_____

Our Experience:
_____
_____
_____
_____
_____
_____

Our Bucket List Goal _____

_____

Date _____ Location _____

Reason of doing this:

_____

_____

_____

_____

Actions we have to take:

_____

_____

_____

_____

_____

_____

Our Experience:

_____

_____

_____

_____

_____

_____

Our Bucket List Goal

Date _____ Location _____

Reason of doing this:

_____
_____
_____
_____

Actions we have to take:

_____
_____
_____
_____
_____
_____

Our Experience:

_____
_____
_____
_____
_____
_____

Our Bucket List Goal ----- ------ ------ -----
----- ------ ------ ------ ------ ------ -----

Date ----- ------ Location ----- ------ -----

Reason of doing this:
----- ------ ------ ------ ------ ------ -----
----- ------ ------ ------ ------ ------ -----
----- ------ ------ ------ ------ ------ -----
----- ------ ------ ------ ------ ------ -----

Actions we have to take:
----- ------ ------ ------ ------ ------ -----
----- ------ ------ ------ ------ ------ -----
----- ------ ------ ------ ------ ------ -----
----- ------ ------ ------ ------ ------ -----
----- ------ ------ ------ ------ ------ -----
----- ------ ------ ------ ------ ------ -----

Our Experience:
----- ------ ------ ------ ------ ------ -----
----- ------ ------ ------ ------ ------ -----
----- ------ ------ ------ ------ ------ -----
----- ------ ------ ------ ------ ------ -----
----- ------ ------ ------ ------ ------ -----

Our Bucket List Goal _____
_____

Date _____ Location _____

Reason of doing this:
_____
_____
_____
_____

Actions we have to take:
_____
_____
_____
_____
_____
_____

Our Experience:
_____
_____
_____
_____
_____
_____

Our Bucket List Goal _____

Date _____   Location _____

Reason of doing this:

_____
_____
_____
_____

Actions we have to take:

_____
_____
_____
_____
_____

Our Experience:

_____
_____
_____
_____
_____

Our Bucket List Goal

Date _ _ _ _ _ _ _ _ _   Location _ _ _ _ _ _ _ _ _

Reason of doing this:

_ _

_ _

_ _

_ _

Actions we have to take:

_ _

_ _

_ _

_ _

_ _

Our Experience:

_ _

_ _

_ _

_ _

_ _

Our Bucket List Goal _____
_____

Date _____ Location _____

Reason of doing this:
_____
_____
_____
_____

Actions we have to take:
_____
_____
_____
_____
_____
_____

Our Experience:
_____
_____
_____
_____
_____
_____

Our Bucket List Goal _____

_____

Date _____ Location _____

Reason of doing this:

_____
_____
_____
_____

Actions we have to take:

_____
_____
_____
_____
_____
_____

Our Experience:

_____
_____
_____
_____
_____
_____

Our Bucket List Goal _____
_____

Date _____ Location _____

Reason of doing this:
_____
_____
_____
_____

Actions we have to take:
_____
_____
_____
_____
_____

Our Experience:
_____
_____
_____
_____
_____

Our Bucket List Goal _____

_____

Date _____ Location _____

Reason of doing this:

_____
_____
_____
_____

Actions we have to take:

_____
_____
_____
_____
_____
_____

Our Experience:

_____
_____
_____
_____
_____
_____

Our Bucket List Goal _____
_____

Date _____ Location _____

Reason of doing this:
_____
_____
_____
_____

Actions we have to take:
_____
_____
_____
_____
_____
_____

Our Experience:
_____
_____
_____
_____
_____
_____

Our Bucket List Goal _____
_____

Date _____ Location _____

Reason of doing this:

Actions we have to take:

Our Experience:

Our Bucket List Goal _____

_____

Date _____ Location _____

Reason of doing this:

_____
_____
_____
_____

Actions we have to take:

_____
_____
_____
_____
_____
_____

Our Experience:

_____
_____
_____
_____
_____
_____

Our Bucket List Goal

_____
_____

Date _____ Location _____

Reason of doing this:

_____
_____
_____
_____

Actions we have to take:

_____
_____
_____
_____
_____
_____

Our Experience:

_____
_____
_____
_____
_____
_____

Our Bucket List Goal

Date _____ Location _____

Reason of doing this:

Actions we have to take:

Our Experience:

Our Bucket List Goal _____

_____

Date _____ Location _____

Reason of doing this:

Actions we have to take:

Our Experience:

Our Bucket List Goal ....
....

Date .... Location ....

Reason of doing this:
....
....
....
....

Actions we have to take:
....
....
....
....
....
....

Our Experience:
....
....
....
....
....
....

Our Bucket List Goal _____

_____

Date _____ Location _____

Reason of doing this:

_____

_____

_____

_____

Actions we have to take:

_____

_____

_____

_____

_____

_____

Our Experience:

_____

_____

_____

_____

_____

_____

Our Bucket List Goal _____

_____

Date _____ Location _____

Reason of doing this:

_____
_____
_____
_____

Actions we have to take:

_____
_____
_____
_____
_____
_____

Our Experience:

_____
_____
_____
_____
_____

Our Bucket List Goal _____

_____

Date _____ Location _____

Reason of doing this:

_____
_____
_____
_____

Actions we have to take:

_____
_____
_____
_____
_____

Our Experience:

_____
_____
_____
_____
_____
_____

Our Bucket List Goal _____
_____

Date _____ Location _____

Reason of doing this:
_____
_____
_____
_____

Actions we have to take:
_____
_____
_____
_____
_____
_____

Our Experience:
_____
_____
_____
_____
_____
_____

Our Bucket List Goal _____

_____

Date _____ Location _____

Reason of doing this:

_____
_____
_____
_____

Actions we have to take:

_____
_____
_____
_____
_____
_____

Our Experience:

_____
_____
_____
_____
_____
_____

Our Bucket List Goal _____

_____

Date _____ Location _____

Reason of doing this:

_____

_____

_____

_____

Actions we have to take:

_____

_____

_____

_____

_____

_____

Our Experience:

_____

_____

_____

_____

_____

Our Bucket List Goal _____

_____

Date _____ Location _____

Reason of doing this:

_____
_____
_____
_____

Actions we have to take:

_____
_____
_____
_____
_____
_____

Our Experience:

_____
_____
_____
_____
_____
_____

Our Bucket List Goal _____

_____

Date _____ Location _____

Reason of doing this:

_____
_____
_____
_____

Actions we have to take:

_____
_____
_____
_____
_____
_____

Our Experience:

_____
_____
_____
_____
_____
_____

Our Bucket List Goal _____

_____

Date _____ Location _____

Reason of doing this:

_____

_____

_____

_____

Actions we have to take:

_____

_____

_____

_____

_____

_____

Our Experience:

_____

_____

_____

_____

_____

_____

Our Bucket List Goal _____

_____

Date _____ Location _____

Reason of doing this:

_____
_____
_____
_____

Actions we have to take:

_____
_____
_____
_____
_____

Our Experience:

_____
_____
_____
_____
_____
_____

Our Bucket List Goal _____

_____

Date _____ Location _____

Reason of doing this:

_____
_____
_____
_____

Actions we have to take:

_____
_____
_____
_____
_____
_____

Our Experience:

_____
_____
_____
_____
_____
_____

Our Bucket List Goal ------------------------

Date ------------------ Location ---------------

Reason of doing this:

Actions we have to take:

Our Experience:

Our Bucket List Goal _____

_____

Date _____ Location _____

Reason of doing this:

_____
_____
_____
_____

Actions we have to take:

_____
_____
_____
_____
_____
_____

Our Experience:

_____
_____
_____
_____
_____
_____

Our Bucket List Goal _____

_____

Date _____ Location _____

Reason of doing this:

_____
_____
_____
_____

Actions we have to take:

_____
_____
_____
_____
_____

Our Experience:

_____
_____
_____
_____
_____

Our Bucket List Goal _____

_____

Date _____ Location _____

Reason of doing this:

_____
_____
_____
_____

Actions we have to take:

_____
_____
_____
_____
_____
_____

Our Experience:

_____
_____
_____
_____
_____
_____

Our Bucket List Goal _____

_____

Date _____ Location _____

Reason of doing this:

_____
_____
_____
_____

Actions we have to take:

_____
_____
_____
_____
_____
_____

Our Experience:

_____
_____
_____
_____
_____
_____

Our Bucket List Goal _____

_____

Date _____ Location _____

Reason of doing this:

_____
_____
_____
_____

Actions we have to take:

_____
_____
_____
_____
_____
_____

Our Experience:

_____
_____
_____
_____
_____
_____

Our Bucket List Goal _____

_____

Date _____ Location _____

Reason of doing this:

_____
_____
_____
_____

Actions we have to take:

_____
_____
_____
_____
_____

Our Experience:

_____
_____
_____
_____
_____

Our Bucket List Goal _____

_____

Date _____ Location _____

Reason of doing this:

Actions we have to take:

Our Experience:

Our Bucket List Goal _____
_____

Date _____   Location _____

Reason of doing this:
_____
_____
_____
_____

Actions we have to take:
_____
_____
_____
_____
_____

Our Experience:
_____
_____
_____
_____
_____

Our Bucket List Goal _____
_____

Date _____ Location _____

Reason of doing this:

Actions we have to take:

Our Experience:

Our Bucket List Goal _____

_____

Date _____ Location _____

Reason of doing this:

_____
_____
_____
_____

Actions we have to take:

_____
_____
_____
_____
_____
_____

Our Experience:

_____
_____
_____
_____
_____
_____

Our Bucket List Goal _____

_____

Date _____ Location _____

Reason of doing this:

_____

_____

_____

_____

Actions we have to take:

_____

_____

_____

_____

_____

_____

Our Experience:

_____

_____

_____

_____

_____

_____

Our Bucket List Goal _____
_____

Date _____ Location _____

Reason of doing this:

Actions we have to take:

Our Experience:

Our Bucket List Goal _____

_____

Date _____ Location _____

Reason of doing this:

_____
_____
_____
_____

Actions we have to take:

_____
_____
_____
_____
_____
_____

Our Experience:

_____
_____
_____
_____
_____
_____

Our Bucket List Goal

_____

_____

Date _____ Location _____

Reason of doing this:

_____
_____
_____
_____

Actions we have to take:

_____
_____
_____
_____
_____
_____

Our Experience:

_____
_____
_____
_____
_____
_____

Our Bucket List Goal ----------------

Date ------------ Location ------------

Reason of doing this:

Actions we have to take:

Our Experience:

Our Bucket List Goal

Date _____ Location _____

Reason of doing this:

_____
_____
_____
_____

Actions we have to take:

_____
_____
_____
_____
_____
_____

Our Experience:

_____
_____
_____
_____
_____

Our Bucket List Goal _____

_____

Date _____ Location _____

Reason of doing this:

_____

_____

_____

_____

Actions we have to take:

_____

_____

_____

_____

_____

_____

Our Experience:

_____

_____

_____

_____

_____

_____

Our Bucket List Goal ....
....

Date .... Location ....

Reason of doing this:

Actions we have to take:

Our Experience:

Our Bucket List Goal _____

_____

Date _____ Location _____

Reason of doing this:

_____
_____
_____
_____

Actions we have to take:

_____
_____
_____
_____
_____
_____

Our Experience:

_____
_____
_____
_____
_____
_____

Our Bucket List Goal _____

_____

Date _____ Location _____

Reason of doing this:

- -
- -
- -
- -

Actions we have to take:

- -
- -
- -
- -
- -
- -

Our Experience:

- -
- -
- -
- -
- -
- -

Our Bucket List Goal _____

_____

Date _____ Location _____

Reason of doing this:

_____

_____

_____

_____

Actions we have to take:

_____

_____

_____

_____

_____

_____

Our Experience:

_____

_____

_____

_____

_____

_____

Our Bucket List Goal _____

_____

Date _____   Location _____

Reason of doing this:

_____
_____
_____
_____

Actions we have to take:

_____
_____
_____
_____
_____
_____

Our Experience:

_____
_____
_____
_____
_____
_____

Our Bucket List Goal _____

_____

Date _____ Location _____

Reason of doing this:

- -
- -
- -
- -

Actions we have to take:

- -
- -
- -
- -
- -
- -

Our Experience:

- -
- -
- -
- -
- -
- -

Our Bucket List Goal _____
_____

Date _____ Location _____

Reason of doing this:
_____
_____
_____
_____

Actions we have to take:
_____
_____
_____
_____
_____
_____

Our Experience:
_____
_____
_____
_____
_____

Our Bucket List Goal _____
_____

Date _____ Location _____

Reason of doing this:
_____
_____
_____
_____

Actions we have to take:
_____
_____
_____
_____
_____
_____

Our Experience:
_____
_____
_____
_____
_____

Our Bucket List Goal ....

....

Date .... Location ....

Reason of doing this:

....
....
....
....

Actions we have to take:

....
....
....
....
....
....

Our Experience:

....
....
....
....
....
....

Our Bucket List Goal _____

_____

Date _____ Location _____

Reason of doing this:

_____
_____
_____
_____

Actions we have to take:

_____
_____
_____
_____
_____
_____

Our Experience:

_____
_____
_____
_____
_____
_____

Our Bucket List Goal _____

_____

Date _____ Location _____

Reason of doing this:

_____
_____
_____
_____

Actions we have to take:

_____
_____
_____
_____
_____
_____

Our Experience:

_____
_____
_____
_____
_____
_____

Our Bucket List Goal

Date _____ Location _____

Reason of doing this:

_____
_____
_____
_____

Actions we have to take:

_____
_____
_____
_____
_____
_____

Our Experience:

_____
_____
_____
_____
_____
_____

Our Bucket List Goal _____

_____

Date _____ Location _____

Reason of doing this:

- -

- -

- -

- -

Actions we have to take:

- -

- -

- -

- -

- -

Our Experience:

- -

- -

- -

- -

- -

Our Bucket List Goal ....

....

Date .... Location ....

Reason of doing this:

....
....
....
....

Actions we have to take:

....
....
....
....
....
....

Our Experience:

....
....
....
....
....
....

Our Bucket List Goal _____
_____

Date _____ Location _____

Reason of doing this:

Actions we have to take:

Our Experience:

Our Bucket List Goal _____

_____

Date _____ Location _____

Reason of doing this:

_____

_____

_____

_____

Actions we have to take:

_____

_____

_____

_____

_____

_____

Our Experience:

_____

_____

_____

_____

_____

Our Bucket List Goal _____

_____

Date _____ Location _____

Reason of doing this:

_____
_____
_____
_____

Actions we have to take:

_____
_____
_____
_____
_____
_____
_____

Our Experience:

_____
_____
_____
_____
_____
_____

Our Bucket List Goal _ _ _ _ _ _ _ _ _ _ _ _ _ _ _
_ _

Date _ _ _ _ _ _ _ _ _ Location _ _ _ _ _ _ _ _ _

Reason of doing this:
_ _
_ _
_ _
_ _

Actions we have to take:
_ _
_ _
_ _
_ _
_ _
_ _

Our Experience:
_ _
_ _
_ _
_ _
_ _
_ _

Our Bucket List Goal _____

_____

Date _____ Location _____

Reason of doing this:

_____
_____
_____
_____

Actions we have to take:

_____
_____
_____
_____
_____
_____

Our Experience:

_____
_____
_____
_____
_____
_____

Our Bucket List Goal _____

_____

Date _____ Location _____

Reason of doing this:

_____

_____

_____

_____

Actions we have to take:

_____

_____

_____

_____

_____

_____

Our Experience:

_____

_____

_____

_____

_____

_____

Our Bucket List Goal _____

_____

Date _____ Location _____

Reason of doing this:

_____
_____
_____
_____

Actions we have to take:

_____
_____
_____
_____
_____
_____

Our Experience:

_____
_____
_____
_____
_____
_____

Our Bucket List Goal _____

_____

Date _____ Location _____

Reason of doing this:

_____
_____
_____
_____

Actions we have to take:

_____
_____
_____
_____
_____
_____

Our Experience:

_____
_____
_____
_____
_____
_____

Our Bucket List Goal _____

_____

Date _____ Location _____

Reason of doing this:

_____
_____
_____
_____

Actions we have to take:

_____
_____
_____
_____
_____
_____

Our Experience:

_____
_____
_____
_____
_____
_____

Our Bucket List Goal

Date _ _ _ _ _ _ _ _ _ Location _ _ _ _ _ _ _ _ _ _

Reason of doing this:

_ _
_ _
_ _
_ _

Actions we have to take:

_ _
_ _
_ _
_ _
_ _
_ _

Our Experience:

_ _
_ _
_ _
_ _
_ _
_ _

Our Bucket List Goal _____

_____

Date _____   Location _____

Reason of doing this:

_____
_____
_____
_____

Actions we have to take:

_____
_____
_____
_____
_____
_____

Our Experience:

_____
_____
_____
_____
_____
_____

Our Bucket List Goal _____

_____

Date _____ Location _____

Reason of doing this:

_____
_____
_____
_____

Actions we have to take:

_____
_____
_____
_____
_____
_____

Our Experience:

_____
_____
_____
_____
_____

Our Bucket List Goal _____

_____

Date _____ Location _____

Reason of doing this:

_____
_____
_____
_____

Actions we have to take:

_____
_____
_____
_____
_____
_____

Our Experience:

_____
_____
_____
_____
_____

Made in the USA
Monee, IL
11 May 2023

33476106R00069